Canning & Preserving Journal

Start Date:_____ End Date:_____

If you are like us, you work year to year perfecting your recipes. This journal will help you make notes from one canning season to the next. You can look back to see how much you put up, so you can judge if you need to can more or less this season.

Happy Canning!
-Lucy & Ethel

Recipe for:
Date:
# of Batches:
Yield:
Method:

RECIPE:

Recipe for:
Date:
# of Batches:
Yield:

Method:

RECIPE:

Recipe for:

Date:

# of Batches:

Yield:

Method:

RECIPE:

Recipe for:
Date:
# of Batches:
Yield:
Method:

RECIPE:

Recipe for:
Date:
# of Batches:
Yield:

Method:

RECIPE:

Recipe for:
Date:
# of Batches:
Yield:

Method:

RECIPE:

Recipe for:
Date:
# of Batches:
Yield:

Method:

RECIPE:

Recipe for:
Date:
# of Batches:
Yield:

Method:

RECIPE:

Recipe for:
Date:
# of Batches:
Yield:

Method:

RECIPE:

Recipe for:
Date:
# of Batches:
Yield:

Method:

RECIPE:

Recipe for:

Date:

# of Batches:

Yield:

Method:

RECIPE:

Recipe for:
Date:
# of Batches:
Yield:

Method:

RECIPE:

Recipe for:
Date:
# of Batches:
Yield:

Method:

RECIPE:

Recipe for:

Date:

# of Batches:

Yield:

Method:

RECIPE:

Recipe for:
Date:
# of Batches:
Yield:
Method:

RECIPE:

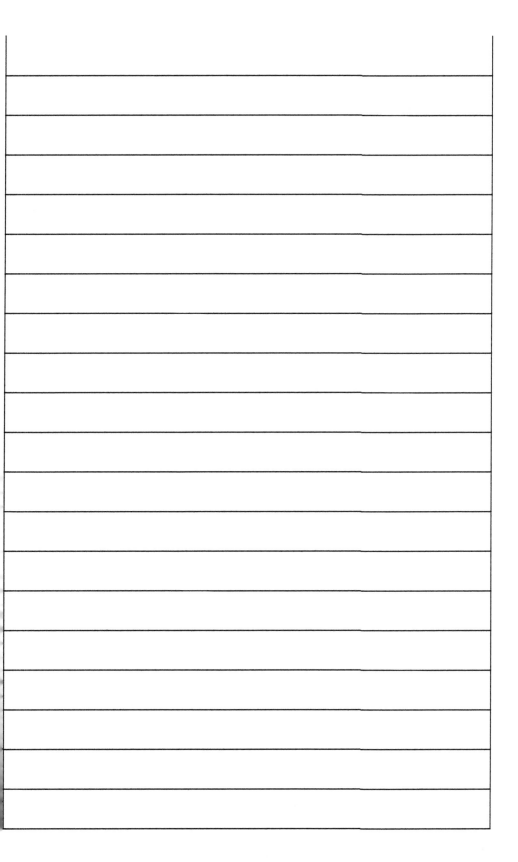

Recipe for:

Date:

# of Batches:

Yield:

Method:

RECIPE:

Recipe for:
Date:
# of Batches:
Yield:

Method:

RECIPE:

Recipe for:

Date:

# of Batches:

Yield:

Method:

RECIPE:

Recipe for:
Date:
# of Batches:
Yield:
Method:

RECIPE:

Recipe for:
Date:
# of Batches:
Yield:
Method:

RECIPE:

Recipe for:

Date:

# of Batches:

Yield:

Method:

RECIPE:

Recipe for:

Date:

# of Batches:

Yield:

Method:

RECIPE:

Recipe for:
Date:
# of Batches:
Yield:

Method:

RECIPE:

Recipe for:
Date:
# of Batches:
Yield:

Method:

RECIPE:

Recipe for:
Date:
# of Batches:
Yield:

Method:

RECIPE:

Recipe for:
Date:
# of Batches:
Yield:

Method:

RECIPE:

Recipe for:
Date:
# of Batches:
Yield:

Method:

RECIPE:

Recipe for:
Date:
# of Batches:
Yield:

Method:

RECIPE:

Recipe for:

Date:

# of Batches:

Yield:

Method:

RECIPE:

Recipe for:
Date:
# of Batches:
Yield:

Method:

RECIPE:

Recipe for:
Date:
# of Batches:
Yield:

Method:

RECIPE:

Recipe for:

Date:

# of Batches:

Yield:

Method:

RECIPE:

Recipe for:
Date:
# of Batches:
Yield:

Method:

RECIPE:

Recipe for:
Date:
# of Batches:
Yield:

Method:

RECIPE:

Recipe for:

Date:

# of Batches:

Yield:

Method:

RECIPE:

Recipe for:
Date:
# of Batches:
Yield:

Method:

RECIPE:

Recipe for:

Date:

# of Batches:

Yield:

Method:

RECIPE:

Recipe for:
Date:
# of Batches:
Yield:
Method:

RECIPE:

Recipe for:

Date:

# of Batches:

Yield:

Method:

RECIPE:

Recipe for:

Date:

# of Batches:

Yield:

Method:

RECIPE:

Recipe for:
Date:
# of Batches:
Yield:

Method:

RECIPE:

Recipe for:
Date:
# of Batches:
Yield:

Method:

RECIPE:

Recipe for:

Date:

# of Batches:

Yield:

Method:

RECIPE:

Recipe for:
Date:
# of Batches:
Yield:
Method:

RECIPE:

Recipe for:
Date:
# of Batches:
Yield:
Method:

RECIPE:

Recipe for:
Date:
# of Batches:
Yield:
Method:

RECIPE:

Recipe for:

Date:

# of Batches:

Yield:

Method:

RECIPE:

Recipe for:
Date:
# of Batches:
Yield:

Method:

RECIPE:

Recipe for:
Date:
# of Batches:
Yield:

Method:

RECIPE:

Canning & Preserving Journal

Start Date:_____ End Date:_____

If you are like us, you work year to year perfecting your recipes. This journal will help you make notes from one canning season to the next. You can look back to see how much you put up, so you can judge if you need to can more or less this season.

Happy Canning!
-Lucy & Ethel

Recipe for:
Date:
# of Batches:
Yield:

Method:

RECIPE:

Recipe for:
Date:
# of Batches:
Yield:

Method:

RECIPE:

Recipe for:

Date:

# of Batches:

Yield:

Method:

RECIPE:

Recipe for:
Date:
# of Batches:
Yield:

Method:

RECIPE:

Recipe for:
Date:
# of Batches:
Yield:

Method:

RECIPE:

Recipe for:
Date:
# of Batches:
Yield:

Method:

RECIPE:

Recipe for:
Date:
# of Batches:
Yield:
Method:

RECIPE:

Recipe for:
Date:
# of Batches:
Yield:
Method:

RECIPE:

Recipe for:
Date:
# of Batches:
Yield:
Method:

RECIPE:

Made in the USA
Middletown, DE
15 November 2022

15090858R00070